How To Build Network Marketing Leader

Step By Step From Newbies To Professional

Introduction

I want to thank you and congratulate you for downloading the book, *"How To Build Network Marketing Leader: Step By Step From Newbies To Professional"*.

This book has actionable strategies on how to build network-marketing leader in a step-by-step formula.

Do you wish to take your network marketing business to the next level? Do you wish you could delegate responsibilities to someone capable of managing your organization successfully, or someone who would not insistently pester you with every contingency? Do you desire to take a break from leading and organizing activities and finally dedicate some quality time to your family without having to worry about the state of your business in your absence?

If you answered these questions with a yes, you're desperately in need of a **network marketing leader.** Yes, a network-marketing leader is the solution to your problems. He or she can help liberate you by managing your business amazingly well.

Unfortunately, finding a capable network-marketing leader is an enormously challenging task. Not everyone is born a leader; but as you well know, you can build a leader from the distributors working within your network marketing business.

Nonetheless, it gets better. You can create; not one, but many remarkable leaders and train them to handle your company like pros, as you have been doing all these years.

Wondering how to accomplish this goal? Well, this book will serve that purpose. Created to help you build professional and extraordinarily capable network marketing leaders, this book contains crucial information you need in order to actualize your objective: **creating remarkable network marketing leaders.**

Thanks again for downloading this book, I hope you enjoy it!

Table of Content

Understanding Network Marketing Companies, Network Marketing Distributors, and Network Marketing Leaders

Before we get started on creating network-marketing leaders, it's essential to highlight some basics right at the beginning. Covering these basics will educate you on differences between a network-marketing distributor and a network-marketing leader. This will place you at a knowledgeable place and allow you insight into why you need the latter.

What is A Network Marketing Company?

A network marketing company is any company working through a network marketing or multilevel marketing model. This type of model helps the business grow by selling its product or service directly to personal contacts, family members, friends, and acquaintances of the entrepreneur as well as the distributors involved in the business.

The upfront investment in this business is usually quite reasonable because anyone can run a network marketing business from a $100 investment. MLM businesses solely depend on a network of marketing distributors responsible for selling products and services. It is the job of the distributors to find prospective clients, market the goods to them, and make sales.

Let's take a peek into the overall responsibilities of a network-marketing distributor and how different they are from those of a networking marketing leader.

Insight: Who are Networking Marketing Distributors, and What Is Their Role?

Network marketing distributors are independent representatives of a company using the network-marketing model. The main job of distributors is to sell the services and products made by MLM Company X. Additionally, a distributor's responsibility is to develop an efficient sales team comprising of professional distributors who can work towards increasing business sales.

Also referred to as multilevel marketing distributors, networking marketing distributors create a proficient marketing strategy and plan that gives the distributors the direction they need to adopt for making sales. Distributors earn a percentage on every sale they make, and from the sales made by their subordinate distributors.

Although distributors are extremely important and crucial to the success of your MLM business, distributors can't help your company reach the pinnacle of success. This is because when a distributor gets a better offer, he or she will cleverly leave your company for the better paying one irrespective of how cemented the relationship may be.

Distributors help in improving your company's success, manage, and organize your company. In case problems arise, they report the problem to you; they lack the courage and expertise needed to resolve the problem on their own. They are devoid of the skills required to propel the company to the next level.

Distributors do not mentor other distributors. They hardly focus on grooming their subordinates and are just concerned about making more money for themselves.

Thus far, we can draw one sharp conclusion: **a distributor's primary concern is him or herself and not your business.**

The goals you've set for your business determine the nature of your business. If your goals are huge, you need someone to help you actualize these goals. Often times, this is not possible with distributors at your disposal. This is where a networking marketing leader comes in. A network-marketing leader can do things a distributor cannot even comprehend.

What, Or, Who Exactly Is A Network Marketing Leader?

A network-marketing leader is a cross between a distributor and a leader. They perform the work of a distributor but go far beyond it to offer more, much more.

Roles of a Network Marketing Leader

Generally, a network-marketing leader has the following responsibilities.

He or she:

Manages all company distributors

Unifies the distributors into one, strong unit

Grooms the distributors and helps them grow by enhancing their capabilities. This can help your company grow by manifolds

Manages time well and doesn't look up to you to solve problems. He or she solves the problem.

Manages tiny and big company tasks

Develops effective marketing plans and works on successfully implementing them

Creates contingency plans to resolve unpredictable issues in a timely and efficient manner

Never complains to, or about the down line distributors

Takes charge of things and ensures everything is executed well

Thinks of your company first and prioritizes company goals

To sum it up, a networking marketing leader is a distributor with well-developed leadership skills. These are skills required for your business to operate harmoniously and in a systematic order. This helps your distributor and customer network to grow, which consequently, boosts company's sales.

To enjoy the hefty benefits offered by a networking marketing leader, you need to find one for your company. However, as indicated earlier, finding an amazing leader is no cakewalk.

Nonetheless, difficult does not in any way mean impossible. In fact, you can create a networking marketing leader or many leaders when you know what it is you are doing.

The rest of this book will outline steps through which you can take capable distributors already in your network, test them, and if you find them capable, turn them into highly capable and competent leaders.

Let's get started with the first step...

Step 1: How to Identify Potential Leaders from Existing Distributors

The first step to building network-marketing leaders in your company is to identify distributors with the potential and talent to become leaders. Becoming a leader isn't easy because it needs a huge amount of courage, skill, confidence, charisma, knowledge, and expertise. Naturally, only a few of your distributors will have an abundance of the above qualities. Therefore, the first thing to do is spot distributors who have leadership skills. So how do you do that? Well, let's take a look at how to make this possible:

How to Identify Potential leaders

Here's how to find out which distributors possess leadership potential.

✓ Look for a Loyal Distributor

Distributors with the potential to become leaders are loyal; their faithfulness never changes. In fact, it doubles in your hour of need because the distributor knows their loyalty is a tool that can help them stay true to the company.

The first thing to look for in a distributor is loyalty towards your company. Search for a distributor who deeply cares for your company and nurture business sentiments similar to ones your business advocate for. This distributor will always remain loyal to your organization, will treat it like their business, and will make its success personal and thus take it up a notch.

To spot loyalty in a distributor, have a chat with some of your best distributors and find out their plans. If their plans revolve around your organization, shortlist them as potential leaders. If not, keep looking for faithful distributors.

✓ Look For an Authoritative yet Compassionate Distributor

Two key characteristics of a leader that help leaders transform something ordinary into extraordinary and lead people to do amazing things are authority and **compassion**. A leader needs to be both, authoritative and compassionate towards their subordinates in order to make them work efficiently and effectively. Therefore, you need to seek these key values in your distributors.

Authority helps the leader influence subordinate distributors so that they listen to the leader and pay heed to their commands. Secondly, being authoritative means the leader has the right expertise and skill needed, and is an expert in their field.

This gives them an upper hand over the rest of the distributors making them fitter to become leaders.

Compassion is important because it makes a leader considerate towards fellow distributors. Kindhearted leaders are concerned about the down line distributors and help them overcome their shortcomings to improve themselves. Hence, it is important to find a distributor who is both an expert and compassionate towards down line distributors.

To identify the right distributor, examine the behavior of all your distributors towards one another, especially the junior distributors. Look for distributors who appreciate fellow distributors, and who can make the most of their skills.

✓ Regular, Punctual, and Organized

A leader knows the value of time; hence, they never waste it. Instead, they use it to the best of their abilities to get more work done in less time. Secondly, they move in an organized manner, ensuring tasks are executed in an orderly fashion with minimal disruptions.

You should seek these characteristics in your distributors. Find distributors that have been doing well since they joined and have maintained or improved their performance. Also, analyze their regularity and look for those who practice the art of time management in getting their chores done. When you spot them, start grooming them.

✓ Are Ambitious and Have a Positive Attitude

Lastly, you need to look for ambition and a positive attitude in your distributors. Leaders are highly ambitious about their goals and have a positive frame of mind, which helps them work harder towards accomplishing their goals. They are enterprising people who possess a winning attitude. They are always striving for better.

While scrutinizing the performance of your network marketing distributors, look for distributors who have clear goals, are super determined to objectify their goals, and have an optimistic attitude. These are the core values of a network-marketing leader.

Now that you know the core characteristics of a network-marketing leader, start the search. It will take time to find a few distributors who can be refined into brilliant leaders. Be focused during the search and only opt for the best distributors. Once, you have shortlisted a few suitable candidates, move on to the next step.

Step2: Set Clear Objectives and Birth Determination

Once you've identified and shortlisted all prospective leaders, embark on molding them into remarkable network marketing leaders. The first thing you need to do is help them set very clear objectives and grow their determination towards achieving or actualizing those goals. You can do that through various ways:

How to Mold Distributors into Potential Leaders

To turn capable distributors into leaders:

✓ Set Clear, Big and Rational Goals

In the first training session, discuss in details with your distributors the goals for your company. State the company goals you aim to achieve, as well as the company mission.

Next, ask individual distributors their goals for themselves and the company. Ask questions such as where they see themselves in five or ten years and what goals they have set for the company in X number of years.

After identifying your company and your distributor's goals and bringing them into the limelight, go through each goal and see if it fits with the company's mission and vision. Next, take the best objectives, polish them, and set them as targets for your company. Write them down and let your distributors know that you want them to believe in these goals and work towards actualizing them; motivate them into believing that from now onwards, those goals are going to be their lifelong goals.

✓ Infuse Motivation

After setting goals for your company, motivate your distributors until these company goals become their goals. For that, you need to let them know how much you value them. Tell them your organization is dependent on them, and it is they who are making it progress smoothly.

Secondly, tell them that you wish for them to become even better and move on to become the future leaders of your network marketing company instead of just distributors. In addition, tell potential leaders of the trust you place in them, and appreciate them for their constant hard work.

An inspirational and emotional talk will definitely stir in them the determination needed to achieve set goals and help them become ambitious. Once they become truly ambitious and determined towards the achievement of company goals, they are not going to hold back and will go beyond the call of duty to objectify these goals.

At this point, you should have a clearer picture of which distributors truly possess the potential to become leaders. After setting clear objectives and ensuring that distributors, cum potential leaders are motivated towards objectifying company goals, the next thing you want to do is_

Step 3: Knowledge Is Key

After a talk with potential leaders, and having them set perfect goals for themselves and your organization, shift to providing your 'leaders-in-waiting' with the knowledge and information they need to become leaders in your marketing company.

Here is how to go about it:

How To Provide Valuable Knowledge To Potential Leaders

✓ Discuss History, Working, and Operations of the Company

Start by educating potential leaders how the network marketing company was started, what obstacles it faced during that time and everything pertinent to its history.

Slowly, move on to discussing how the company evolved and changed with time as well as its current mode of operation. Make sure to highlight milestones the organization has achieved so far, along with its annual profit, revenue, and details of its employees. Discuss every aspect of the company with the distributors to help them know and understand the business in an in-depth manner. This will help them know the company well and assist them develop effective marketing strategies.

✓ Create SWOT and PEST Analyses

Once orientation to your marketing company is complete, together with your select few distributors, create SWOT and PEST analyses of the company.

SWOT stands for **S**trength, **W**eaknesses, **O**pportunities, and **T**hreats. SWOT analyses allow you insight into external factors that affect the company. This in turn helps you become aware of all the strong points, weaknesses and issues faced by a company.

On the other hand, the PEST analysis informs you of different elements that positively or negatively affect your business. Both analyses help you devise tactful and effective strategies to make your company better, efficient, and more profitable.

Ask distributors to create these analyses and then devise suitable marketing plans accordingly. Of course, you must help them out, so their goals and plans align and are parallel to yours.

✓ Advanced Technology and its Benefits

Next, discuss the latest technological applications and inventions that can help your company in any possible manner. Discuss the different technological inventions you think can help your network marketing company run better and smoothly and ask for their input.

Communicate your research with potential leaders and ask each to carry out independent research on the subject and create a report. This makes them feel involved and helps them create beneficial strategies for your company.

✓ Discuss the Competitors

Lastly, you need to give them elaborated information on your competitors. Talk to them about how well or poorly the competitors are performing and the strategies they employ to achieve success.

During this discussion, examine the input given by different distributors. Well-informed and efficient distributors will know of 80 to 90 percent of the information you are giving them and will probably have more to add to it. Be on the lookout for these distributors; they're the ones who care enough for your company to go out of their way to discover beneficial information about it and its competition.

Once you've provided potential leaders with all information related to different aspects of the business as discussed above, you are free to move on to the next step.

Step 4: Teach Potential Leaders Management and Leadership Skills

'People ask the difference between a leader and a boss. The leader leads, and the boss drives.'

- Theodore Roosevelt

Do you see the simple, meaningful quote above? It talks about the most important quality of a leader. A leader is one who leads, whereas a boss merely a person who drives and manages. To develop and create leaders out of your best distributors, your next task is to teach them how to manage things and not people because most people need someone to lead so they can follow.

Difference between Leading and Managing People

For starters, there are unique differences between leading and managing people. Managing people, in this case, down line distributors and other workers means making sure workers follow directives.

When managing people, trying to assert great control over them does not work because it's too intrusive. Most distributors don't like being dominated or talked to harshly. Therefore, managing people will never help achieve desired results. What your leaders need to do is to lead.

Leading subordinate distributors and staff members means providing a clear path and directions to follow. Set examples for your leaders and motivate them to follow these examples so that they can strive to be better, and consequently benefit the company. Leadership is not about compelling others to do something. Rather, it is about motivating them to achieve set goals. Once you feel your distributors understand this, you should move forward.

How to Teach Potential Leaders Leadership Skills

Together with your leaders, discuss how to lead people, i.e. how to go about leading others. For starters, clearly discuss the need to become approachable so that others find them polite to talk to and easy to discuss their problems with. Only then, will you be able to enhance their skills.

Thirdly, your leaders need to lose the authoritative tone in their voice and become eloquent. Fourthly, tell leaders not to force anybody into doing something. Instead, they should learn to motivate others by rewarding those who do well. This will motivate others to exert more effort.

Additionally, your potential leaders need to practice whatever they preach to their down line distributors. This will show other distributors that their leader is true to his or her words and principles and does what he or she says. This will influence junior distributors and make it easier for them to follow their leadership.

Once you have communicated these things to potential leaders, talk to them about the importance of managing different aspects of their work and business.

How to Teach Your Leaders Management Skills

Discuss with your leaders the importance of management. Most people tend to need leadership and management to ensure the company moves forward smoothly and takes steps leading to prosperity. To manage, potential network-marketing leads must learn to organize themselves and everything around them, so things become systematic and orderly.

Here are the different things potential leaders need to do to become effective.

Firstly, ask them to create files for different company documents relative to the products available. Each product category and aspect needs to be filed separately and every file must contain relevant documents. Choose distributors who have maintained this system, appreciate them, and keep studying them because they can be the leaders you are seeking.

Secondly, ask your 'leaders-in-waiting' to make a list of all tasks that have been executed well, those being processed, and the ones that need to be carried out in the future. This will help them divide all the jobs into different categories and help them create time and actionable plans for their achievement.

Thirdly, ask your leaders to organize their offices and ensure everything is in order. This will help them find things on time and work on tasks conveniently.

Once you you're done with this step, ask them to start implementing the guidelines and examine their actions. See which distributor pays heed to your guidelines and who doesn't to know which candidates can become future leaders in your network marketing company.

Step 5: Instill Growth in Your Leaders-In-Waiting

The next step to creating leaders off your distributors list is the need to let your distributors i.e. leaders to grow. As they grow, they should allow their down line distributors to do the same.

There are many ways to go about cultivating significant growth in your leaders and allow them to do the same with their down line.

How to Cultivate Crazy growth in Potential leaders

Here is what you need to do to groom your leaders.

1. *Appreciate their Strengths*

For starters, appreciate their amazing work and strengths. Analyze individual distributors to find out their strengths. Next, let each distributor know how much he or she means to you and the company, praise him or her for their amazing effort and point out their unique strengths. Don't just dish out empty appreciations. Appreciation is an emotional human need and when you give it to others, it motivates them into being better in every way possible. Appreciate your best distributors i.e. leaders who are now in training, to make them more faithful towards the company.

2. *Work on their Weaknesses*

Secondly, help your leaders-in-training work towards overcoming their weaknesses and polishing their skills. Have individual discussions with each leader-in-training and discuss techniques to convert that specific leader's shortcomings into strengths or eliminate the weaknesses. This will help you curate highly capable leaders.

3. *Mentor Them*

Additionally, cultivate a 'mentor-mentee' relationship with your leaders-in-incubation. This will greatly assist in fostering effective communication, and allow you a chance to continue mentoring them. However, if you feel a distributor respects you, but has another mentor, then do not ask him to change that. You must give your leaders freedom to be themselves and idolize whoever they want as long as they are loyal to you. They can learn beneficial things from other mentors and use it to your advantage.

4. Delegate Authority

Finally, delegate authority to your leaders. Your leaders-in-training need to have authority to do things on their own without running every idea or task by you before implementing it.

They need to feel that they own this company for them to become truly involved and interested in it, which is why you must give them charge over important tasks. Most capable leaders will make mistakes, learn from their errors, and emerge confident and better distributors who can become leaders in your company.

5. Ask them to do the same with their Subordinates

While grooming the potential list of leaders from your distributors, ask them to groom their down line distributors. This will ensure that their subordinates develop into better distributors. With more refined and productive distributors, your chances of having more leaders increase. Therefore, ensure your distributors let their subordinates grow and develop.

Step 6: Improve Their Efficiency

After instilling growth in your potential leaders, the next thing in line is helping your distributors become more efficient and productive because leaders are highly productive and efficient.

A leader knows how best to use his or her time to improve productivity. To turn gifted distributors into brilliant leaders, you must boost their efficiency.

How To Improve Efficiency In Leaders-In-Training

To increase efficiency in your leaders, here are the skills you must teach them.

✓ Time Management

Leaders must know, understand, and comprehend the art of time management because they cannot become productive until they know how to use their time.

Teach your leaders effective time management. Firstly, tell them to stop delaying the most important tasks and start working on them instantly. Procrastination is a monster that can hinder goals and objective achievement, which is why your leaders need to eliminate it from their lives if they want to become the leaders of the company.

Next, ask potential leaders to minimize distractions and attend only to important calls when working. Thirdly, ask them to install helpful time management apps such as Rescue Time, Stay Focusd, Dropbox, and Focus Booster on their laptops and phones. This will go far in helping potential leaders become better at effective time management.

Fourthly, discuss the 80-20 rule or Pareto Principle with them. This rule dictates that by exerting about 20 percent of your effort at the right time and with the right techniques, you can achieve around 80 percent of your desired results. Ask your leaders-in-waiting to identify their peak energy times and work on finding the right techniques to accomplish things during this time so they can enjoy greater results. Leaders must learn how to prioritize tasks by differentiating between important and less important tasks and working on less important tasks only after completing important tasks. Finally, motivate them to implement these tactics, so they can exercise time management and improve their current efficiency.

✓ Selective Focus

Teach potential leaders the selective focus skill to boost their concentration. As their concentration improves, they will become more attentive to their work and come up with amazing solutions to pressing issues.

For that to happen, your leaders must learn how to focus selectively on important things. Ask your distributors cum leaders to practice deep breathing when they need to focus, count to five when inhaling and relax when exhaling. This will instill in them the confidence they need to become truly focused and determined leaders.

Next, ask potential leaders to think and focus on one task at a time and readjust their focus when they experience distractions. With constant practice, they will be able to increase their attention span and focus, which will enhance their performance largely.

✓ Become Punctual and Responsible

To become efficient and amazing leaders, your distributors need to become responsible, mature, and punctual. A leader is punctual, regular, and prompt. They are never late to work because they know they have people to lead and tasks to carry out.

Moreover, leaders are aware of their responsibilities and know the tasks they need to handle, which is why they never procrastinate and are always working hard to complete important tasks. For distributors to become great leaders, they need to become punctual, responsible, and mature.

Teach them how to develop a morning routine that ensures that they start working on time and stay focused on the job. You should also teach them how to nurture the habit of getting things done when they should be done and only leaving after completing all the scheduled tasks for the day. Additionally, teach potential distributors to be available to you and other concerned people 24/7 via phone, email, or even social media. This helps you connect to them easily and promptly, which ensures important tasks are completed properly, and on time.

To become mature and responsible, your list of potential leaders must take charge of duties assigned to them and avoid pestering you with constant complaints. They should know how to handle problems on their own, not complain to others, and always refrain from speaking ill of others. This makes them mature; when they become sensible, they become more focused and responsible.

After conveying these messages to your small list of gifted distributors, remind them to implement these guidelines. Remind them that these guidelines will increase their efficiency and help them become network-marketing leaders in your company.

Step 7: Discuss the Significance of Favors

The last step to creating effective network-marketing leaders is polishing your distributors. Polishing your leaders will change them into the fantastic leaders you've been looking for.

To achieve this, discuss with your 'leaders-awaiting-graduation' the importance of favors in networking.

In this regard, discuss how to:

✓ Give Favors to Receive Favors

Multilevel marketing revolves around creating effective networks. To create networks, there's need to be tactful. People in this business are drawn towards you when they know you can benefit them in one way or the other.

Therefore, generously give favors to those who can help you in return. Teach your distributors the importance of helping out others, especially those in power. This ability will turn them into powerful and influential leaders.

A leader knows how best to use his or her resources and knows what to invest in order to accomplish their goals. For distributors to become excellent leaders, they need to reach out to people and grant them different favors, so these people will feel obliged to return the favor should the need arise. Giving favors is a good trick to influence people especially because it makes people to feel indebted to you.

Tell your potential leaders personal stories to help them understand the importance of favors. Tell them how you benefitted from the strengths of others simply by offering favors when someone was in dire need of one. However, leaders must learn to weigh the pros and cons of dolling out favors to all and sundry.

Conclusion

The key to success in network marketing lies in building great network marketing leaders. The information contained herein provides you with guidelines you can use to create highly effective network-marketing leaders.

Encourage your distributors cum leaders to exercise each of the seven steps we have outlined here and continuously review their performance. Be patient, it may take a few months to practice all the guidelines. During the implementation stage, identify the best performers and make the network-marketing leaders in your MLM Company.

Thank you again for downloading this book!

I hope this book was able to help you to understand how best to develop an abled team of network marketing leaders.

The next step is to implement what you've just learnt.

Finally, if you enjoyed this book, would you be kind enough to leave a review for this book on Amazon?

Click here to leave a review for this book on Amazon!

Thank you and good luck!